Bible Memory Word Searches for Kids

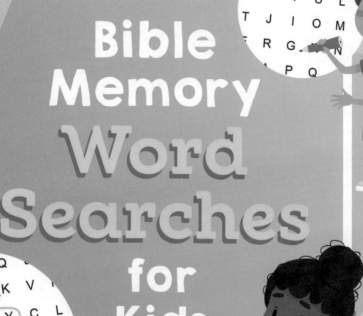

BARBOUR **kidz**

A Division of Barbour Publishing

Published by Barbour Publishing, Inc., 1810 Barbour Drive, Uhrichsville, Ohio 44683, www.barbourbooks.com

Our mission is to inspire the world with the life-changing message of the Bible.

Member of the
Evangelical Christian
Publishers Association

Printed in China.
001376 1022 XY

HEY, KIDS!

Here are 40 fantastically fun word search puzzles for your enjoyment!

You'll find search words highlighted in short Bible verses you can memorize, all of them taken from the easy-to-understand New Life Version.

Find the special words in the puzzle while you hide God's Word in your heart!

And if you get stuck, answer pages are in the back of the book.

Grab your pencil. . .and get ready to begin your very own Bible-memory word-search adventure!

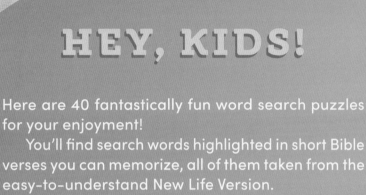

PUZZLE 1

What does the Bible say about pleasing God?

1

A man cannot please God unless he has faith.

HEBREWS 11:6

2

If I were still trying to please men, I would not be a servant owned by Christ.

GALATIANS 1:10

3

God has allowed us to be trusted with the Good News. Because of this, we preach it to please God, not man.

1 THESSALONIANS 2:4

4

When the ways of a man are pleasing to the Lord, He makes even those who hate him to be at peace with him.

PROVERBS 16:7

5

Those who do what their sinful old selves want to do cannot please God.

ROMANS 8:8

6

Do not act like the sinful people of the world. Let God change your life.

ROMANS 12:2

7

We will receive from Him whatever we ask if we obey Him and do what He wants.

1 JOHN 3:22

8

Remember to do good and help each other. Gifts like this please God.

HEBREWS 13:16

9

So if we stay here on earth or go home to Him, we always want to please Him.

2 CORINTHIANS 5:9

10

Then Peter and the missionaries said, "We must obey God instead of men!"

ACTS 5:29

Find These Words in the Puzzle!

FAITH   PEACE   GOOD

SERVANT   PLEASE   HOME

PREACH   LIFE   GOD

              OBEY

```
K  R  K  N  T  D  F  N  M  N
P  V  R  H  Z  M  H  Q  N  N
L  P  X  T  R  Y  L  Z  G  F
E  K  E  I  N  L  D  T  E  V
A  N  M  A  I  Q  N  O  M  Y
S  J  B  F  C  A  Q  L  O  K
E  M  E  D  V  E  N  Z  H  G
R  F  O  R  M  W  N  M  V  L
X  G  E  P  R  E  A  C  H  W
P  S  Y  H  R  J  Y  E  B  O
```

PUZZLE 2

What does the Bible say about loving others?

1

"If you love each other, all men will know you are My followers."
JOHN 13:35

2

Whoever loves his brother is in the light. And there will be no reason to sin because of him.
1 JOHN 2:10

3

My children, let us not love with words or in talk only. Let us love by what we do and in truth.
1 JOHN 3:18

4

Those who love are God's children and they know God.
1 JOHN 4:7

5

You do not need anyone to write to you about loving your Christian brothers. God has taught you to love each other.
1 THESSALONIANS 4:9

6

Dear friends, if God loved us that much, then we should love each other.
1 JOHN 4:11

7

"Do not hurt someone who has hurt you. Do not keep on hating the sons of your people, but love your neighbor as yourself."
LEVITICUS 19:18

8

Do not owe anyone anything, but love each other. Whoever loves his neighbor has done what the Law says to do.
ROMANS 13:8

9

"Do for other people whatever you would like to have them do for you."
MATTHEW 7:12

10

We have these words from Him. If you love God, love your brother also.
1 JOHN 4:21

Find These Words in the Puzzle!

LOVE   KNOW   LAW

LIGHT   TAUGHT   PEOPLE

TRUTH   GOD   BROTHER

                     NEIGHBOR

```
H E X M G R M K R M
T L Q T Q G X L C P
A P R Z O V M K R E
U O K D R T C E X V
G E H N H W H M N O
H P L G O T A P B L
T D I M O W P L D P
K L T R U T H Z L Y
Q N B M Z M D F J V
D R O B H G I E N R
```

PUZZLE 3

What does the Bible say about worrying?

1

Do not worry. Learn to pray about everything. Give thanks to God as you ask Him for what you need.

PHILIPPIANS 4:6

2

Give all your worries to Him because He cares for you.

1 PETER 5:7

3

God is our safe place and our strength. He is always our help when we are in trouble.

PSALM 46:1

4

He will call upon Me, and I will answer him. I will be with him in trouble.

PSALM 91:15

5

"Do not let your heart be troubled. You have put your trust in God, put your trust in Me also."

JOHN 14:1

6

"Do not worry about your life, what you are going to eat. Do not worry about your body, what you are going to wear."

LUKE 12:22

7

I looked for the Lord, and He answered me. And He took away all my fears.

PSALM 34:4

8

Trust in the Lord with all your heart, and do not trust in your own understanding.

PROVERBS 3:5

9

Worry in the heart of a man weighs it down, but a good word makes it glad.

PROVERBS 12:25

10

When I am afraid, I will trust in You.

PSALM 56:3

Find These Words in the Puzzle!

PRAY   TROUBLE   LORD

WORRIES   HEART   WEIGHS

SAFE   LIFE   AFRAID

                 FEARS

S	R	H	W	S	A	F	E	H	Y
H	S	R	A	E	F	M	Q	E	Y
G	P	G	R	L	L	L	P	A	A
I	T	X	T	I	V	S	M	R	R
E	R	R	F	M	E	B	D	T	P
W	C	E	O	I	D	I	D	G	M
K	T	V	R	U	A	R	J	B	K
N	T	R	Y	R	B	J	O	B	Y
N	O	L	F	N	W	L	K	L	R
W	N	A	K	N	M	Y	E	D	X

PUZZLE 4

What does the Bible say about having joy?

1

You have filled my heart with more happiness than they have when there is much grain and wine.
PSALM 4:7

2

Yet I will have joy in the Lord. I will be glad in the God Who saves me.
HABAKKUK 3:18

3

For our heart is full of joy in Him, because we trust in His holy name.
PSALM 33:21

4

"Do not be sad for the joy of the Lord is your strength."
NEHEMIAH 8:10

5

"You are sad now. I will see you again and then your hearts will be full of joy."
JOHN 16:22

6

"I have told you these things so My joy may be in you and your joy may be full."
JOHN 15:11

7

Those who plant with tears will gather fruit with songs of joy.
PSALM 126:5

8

"Until now you have not asked for anything in My name. Ask and you will receive. Then your joy will be full."
JOHN 16:24

9

For the holy nation of God is not food and drink. It is being right with God. I.t is peace and joy given by the Holy Spirit.
ROMANS 14:17

10

Be full of joy always because you belong to the Lord. Again I say, be full of joy!
PHILIPPIANS 4:4

Find These Words in the Puzzle!

HAPPINESS   STRENGTH   ASKED
SAVES   SAD   SPIRIT
TRUST   FULL   LORD
             SONGS

```
D  Z  P  T  R  U  S  T  R  X
H  Y  T  C  M  E  I  S  V  N
T  L  N  K  V  R  H  S  C  R
G  M  L  A  I  L  S  E  L  P
N  P  S  P  S  O  K  N  T  K
E  D  S  V  N  A  J  I  K  K
R  F  R  G  R  N  D  P  N  H
T  U  S  O  H  M  F  P  T  R
S  L  P  N  L  F  G  A  K  R
X  L  D  E  K  S  A  H  Y  T
```

1

Do not be quick in spirit to be angry. For anger is in the heart of fools.
ECCLESIASTES 7:9

2

He who is slow to anger is better than the powerful. And he who rules his spirit is better than he who takes a city.
PROVERBS 16:32

3

Stop being angry. Turn away from fighting. Do not trouble yourself. It leads only to wrong-doing.
PSALM 37:8

4

If you are angry, do not let it become sin. Get over your anger before the day is finished.
EPHESIANS 4:26

5

"But I tell you that whoever is angry with his brother will be guilty and have to suffer for his wrong-doing."
MATTHEW 5:22

6

Christian brothers, never pay back someone for the bad he has done to you. Let the anger of God take care of the other person.
ROMANS 12:19

7

If the one who hates you is hungry, feed him. If he is thirsty, give him water.
PROVERBS 25:21

8

A fool always loses his temper, but a wise man keeps quiet.
PROVERBS 29:11

9

A man's anger does not allow him to be right with God.
JAMES 1:20

10

Put out of your life these things also: anger, bad temper, bad feelings toward others, talk that hurts people, speaking against God, and dirty talk.
COLOSSIANS 3:8

Find These Words in the Puzzle!

QUICK
RULES
FIGHTING

SIN
GUILTY
PAY
FEED

WISE
ANGER
TEMPER

```
R N P H E W S P R K
N A Q L R S M I C F
Y D E E F K I H N X
H R G X R C T W P M
W F U D E I V C S R
L H I T G U Q E E F
X Q L G N Q L P M R
H T T R A U M J N B
Y P Y H R E V N H F
F I G H T I N G Y J
```

PUZZLE 6

What does the Bible say about being happy with what you have?

1

Everyone should live the life the Lord gave to him. He should live as he was when he became a Christian.
1 CORINTHIANS 7:17

2

A God-like life gives us much when we are happy for what we have.
1 TIMOTHY 6:6

3

Do not let your heart be jealous of sinners, but live in the fear of the Lord always.
PROVERBS 23:17

4

"Watch yourselves! Keep from wanting all kinds of things you should not have. A man's life is not made up of things."
LUKE 12:15

5

A little earned in a right way is better than much earned in a wrong way.
PROVERBS 16:8

6

A poor man who walks in his honor is better than a rich man who is sinful in his ways.
PROVERBS 28:6

7

And my God will give you everything you need because of His great riches in Christ Jesus.
PHILIPPIANS 4:19

8

I am not saying I need anything. I have learned to be happy with whatever I have.
PHILIPPIANS 4:11

9

The Lord is my Shepherd. I will have everything I need.
PSALM 23:1

10

"Those who are hungry and thirsty to be right with God are happy, because they will be filled."
MATTHEW 5:6

Find These Words in the Puzzle!

CHRISTIAN
MUCH
JEALOUS

WATCH
RIGHT
HONOR
EVERYTHING

NEED
SHEPHERD
FILLED

```
G W N K K F H R R F
N P A V H C K I D I
I B I T U Z H G Z L
H K T M C O L H X L
T N S C N H W T Z E
Y J I O M K F T L D
R D R E H P E H S Q
E J H J E A L O U S
V V C N R R Y M X N
E J D E E N V M L P
```

PUZZLE 7

What does the Bible say about Jesus Christ?

1

The Word (Christ) was in the beginning. The Word was with God. The Word was God.

JOHN 1:1

2

"You will give Him the name Jesus because He will save His people from the punishment of their sins."

MATTHEW 1:21

3

Jesus grew strong in mind and body. He grew in favor with God and men.

LUKE 2:52

4

Those in the boat worshiped Jesus. They said, "For sure, You are the Son of God!"

MATTHEW 14:33

5

Simon Peter said, "You are the Christ, the Son of the living God."

MATTHEW 16:16

6

A voice came from heaven and said, "You are My much-loved Son. I am very happy with You."

MARK 1:11

7

The Law was given through Moses, but loving-favor and truth came through Jesus Christ.

JOHN 1:17

8

Jesus walked by. John looked at Him and said, "See! The Lamb of God."

JOHN 1:36

9

God lifted Jesus high above everything else. He gave Him a name that is greater than any other name.

PHILIPPIANS 2:9

10

"There is no other name under heaven given to men by which we can be saved."

ACTS 4:12

Find These Words in the Puzzle!

WORD   WORSHIPED   LAMB
JESUS   LIVING   NAME
FAVOR   SON   SAVED
              TRUTH

Q N D S J J H M L N
K P R O L P W N D S
R H O N C G R E U T
L T W V G Q V S R N
K I W C W A E U D E
X F V H S J T F L M
R T X I M H B M T A
Z N R W N C T M T N
F A V O R G X D A J
D E P I H S R O W L

PUZZLE 8

What does the Bible say about being honest?

1

"Do not steal. Be honest in what you do. Do not *lie* to one another."
LEVITICUS 19:11

2

Do not lie to each other. You have put out of your life your *old* ways.
COLOSSIANS 3:9

3

A man who tells lies about someone will be *punished*. He who tells lies will not get away.
PROVERBS 19:5

4

I hate what is *false*, but I love Your Law.
PSALM 119:163

5

The Lord hates lying lips, but those who speak the *truth* are His joy.
PROVERBS 12:22

6

A *faithful* man who tells what he knows will not lie, but the man who is not faithful will lie.
PROVERBS 14:5

7

Take lies and what is false *far* from me.
PROVERBS 30:8

8

Stop lying to each other. Tell the truth to your neighbor. We all belong to the same *body*.
EPHESIANS 4:25

9

"Do not tell a lie about your *neighbor*."
EXODUS 20:16

10

He who speaks the truth tells what is *right*, but a liar tells lies.
PROVERBS 12:17

Find These Words in the Puzzle

LIE
OLD
PUNISHED

FALSE
TRUTH
FAITHFUL
FAR

BODY
NEIGHBOR
RIGHT

L	R	O	B	H	G	I	E	N	T
R	A	F	L	K	B	N	Y	B	R
P	U	N	I	S	H	E	D	F	U
R	K	M	M	P	K	Y	A	D	T
T	N	K	F	D	V	I	L	P	H
T	K	F	Z	A	T	O	F	L	T
Z	Y	R	T	H	L	H	N	X	H
X	W	D	F	V	C	S	J	E	G
N	R	U	O	L	J	B	E	I	I
Y	L	K	K	B	N	R	L	L	R

PUZZLE 9

What does the Bible say about kids?

1

Children, *obey* your parents in everything. The Lord is pleased when you do.
COLOSSIANS 3:20

2

"Whoever does not receive the holy nation of God as a little *child* does not go into it."
MARK 10:15

3

Jesus said, "Let the little children come to Me. Do not stop them. The holy nation of *heaven* is made up of ones like these."
MATTHEW 19:14

4

He took the children in His arms. He put His hands on them and prayed that *good* would come to them.
MARK 10:16

5

Out of the *mouth* of children and babies, You have built up strength.
PSALM 8:2

6

"Be sure you do not hate one of these little children. I tell you, they have angels who are always looking into the face of My *Father* in heaven."
MATTHEW 18:10

7

See, children are a *gift* from the Lord.
PSALM 127:3

8

"Every one of you must have *respect* for his mother and his father."
LEVITICUS 19:3

9

My son, keep the *teaching* of your father, and do not turn away from the teaching of your mother.
PROVERBS 6:20

10

"Whoever *receives* one of these little children in My name, receives Me."
MARK 9:37

Find These Words in the Puzzle!

OBEY

CHILD

HEAVEN

GOOD

MOUTH

FATHER

GIFT

RESPECT

TEACHING

RECEIVES

J	H	G	X	D	K	N	P	L	G
K	V	P	L	L	T	L	S	G	X
T	G	I	H	E	A	V	E	N	Y
R	H	O	T	T	F	J	V	I	T
C	E	K	O	A	L	Y	I	H	Y
T	L	S	T	D	X	E	E	C	M
R	T	H	P	T	L	B	C	A	O
M	E	Q	P	E	K	O	E	E	U
R	T	F	I	G	C	N	R	T	T
F	J	C	W	G	V	T	Y	M	H

PUZZLE 10

What does the Bible say about God's kindness?

1

The Lord has loving-pity on those who fear Him, as a father has loving-pity on his children.
PSALM 103:13

2

Let us thank the God and Father of our Lord Jesus Christ. It was through His loving-kindness that we were born again to a new life.
1 PETER 1:3

3

It is because of the Lord's loving-kindness that we are not destroyed for His loving-pity never ends.
LAMENTATIONS 3:22

4

You will give me goodness and loving-kindness all the days of my life. Then I will live with You in Your house forever.
PSALM 23:6

5

It was not because we worked to be right with God. It was because of His loving-kindness that He washed our sins away.
TITUS 3:5

6

Remember Your loving-pity and Your loving-kindness, O Lord. For they have been from old.
PSALM 25:6

7

God said to Moses, "I will have loving-kindness and loving-pity for anyone I want to."
ROMANS 9:15

8

For You are good and ready to forgive, O Lord. You are rich in loving-kindness to all who call to You.
PSALM 86:5

9

The Lord is good to all. And His loving-kindness is over all His works.
PSALM 145:9

10

Who is a God like You? . . . He does not stay angry forever because He is happy to show loving-kindness.
MICAH 7:18

Find These Words in the Puzzle!

FATHER   FOREVER   RICH
LIFE   WASHED   GOOD
NEVER   OLD   HAPPY
              MOSES

L	W	M	F	G	M	O	T	H	D
N	A	H	X	O	L	M	M	L	O
R	S	L	C	D	R	K	L	M	O
C	H	L	R	I	R	E	E	Q	G
S	E	S	O	M	R	F	V	R	Q
B	D	N	C	M	I	Z	D	E	P
F	L	H	Z	L	L	M	R	H	R
N	N	E	V	E	R	C	H	T	P
Y	P	P	A	H	M	M	R	A	T
L	L	R	N	B	T	V	N	F	R

PUZZLE II

What does the Bible say about being proud?

1

Pride comes before being destroyed and a proud spirit comes before a fall.
PROVERBS 16:18

2

It is bad for those who are wise in their own eyes, and who think they know a lot!
ISAIAH 5:21

3

Do you see a man who is wise in his own eyes? There is more hope for a fool than for him.
PROVERBS 26:12

4

You speak sharp words to the proud, the hated ones, because they turn from Your Word.
PSALM 119:21

5

Let another man praise you, and not your own mouth. Let a stranger, and not your own lips.
PROVERBS 27:2

6

If anyone wants to be proud, he should be proud of what the Lord has done.
2 CORINTHIANS 10:17

7

Eyes lifted high and a proud heart is sin and is the lamp of the sinful.
PROVERBS 21:4

8

"Proud," "Self-important" and "One who laughs at the truth" are the names of the man who acts without respect and is proud.
PROVERBS 21:24

9

A man's pride will bring him down, but he whose spirit is without pride will receive honor.
PROVERBS 29:23

10

Live in peace with each other. Do not act or think with pride.
ROMANS 12:16

Find These Words in the Puzzle!

DESTROYED   SHARP   RESPECT
WISE   STRANGER   DOWN
FOOL   LORD   PEACE
                LAMP

P Z K T H P K Q H B
D N S D C K J N W E
S H T E L E P M S K
M H R Y J G P I Y Q
Q P A O X B W S M L
K N N R T L E L E J
L W G T P C O C X R
B O E S A R F O O L
C D R E D Z M T Q N
F K P D J P M A L N

PUZZLE 12

What does the Bible say about being brave?

1

He gives strength to the weak. And He gives power to him who has little strength.
ISAIAH 40:29

2

Be strong. Be strong in heart, all you who hope in the Lord.
PSALM 31:24

3

"Do not be afraid. For those who are with us are more than those who are with them."
2 KINGS 6:16

4

"Be strong and have strength of heart. Do not be afraid or shake with fear because of them. For the Lord your God is the One Who goes with you."
DEUTERONOMY 31:6

5

Watch and keep awake! Stand true to the Lord. Keep on acting like men and be strong.
1 CORINTHIANS 16:13

6

"Do not fear, for I am with you. Do not be afraid, for I am your God. I will give you strength, and for sure I will help you."
ISAIAH 41:10

7

For God did not give us a spirit of fear. He gave us a spirit of power and of love and of a good mind.
2 TIMOTHY 1:7

8

"Be strong. Let us show ourselves to have strength of heart."
2 SAMUEL 10:12

9

"But you be strong. Do not lose strength of heart. For you will be paid for your work."
2 CHRONICLES 15:7

10

At once Jesus spoke to them and said, "Take hope. It is I. Do not be afraid!"
MATTHEW 14:27

Find These Words in the Puzzle!

POWER   SHAKE   STRENGTH
HOPE   AWAKE   PAID
MORE   GOD   JESUS
               SPIRIT

F L F Z P R R R H G
N T I R I P S G T A
R H P M M F O N G W
G V D E K D H F N A
D S P I S W R R E K
C O H U A M E V R E
H Z S A W P W T T B
T E J N K K O P S D
J M G W C E P G K M
L M O R E V C L K X

PUZZLE 13

How does the Bible say we should treat our enemies?

1

"I say to you who hear Me, love those who work against you. Do good to those who hate you."
LUKE 6:27

2

"Pray for those who do bad things to you and who make it hard for you."
MATTHEW 5:44

3

Pray and give thanks for those who make trouble for you. Yes, pray for them instead of talking against them.
ROMANS 12:14

4

"If the one who hates you is hungry, feed him. If he is thirsty, give him water."
ROMANS 12:20

5

Then Jesus said, "Father, forgive them. They do not know what they are doing."
LUKE 23:34

6

When someone does something bad to you, do not do the same thing to him. When someone talks about you, do not talk about him. Instead, pray that good will come to him.
1 PETER 3:9

7

Love does not get angry. Love does not remember the suffering that comes from being hurt by someone.
1 CORINTHIANS 13:5

8

Do not be full of joy when the one who hates you falls. Do not let your heart be glad when he trips.
PROVERBS 24:17

9

"If you love those who love you, what reward can you expect from that? Do not even the tax-gatherers do that?"
MATTHEW 5:46

10

Hate starts fights, but love covers all sins.
PROVERBS 10:12

Find These Words in the Puzzle!

AGAINST HUNGRY FALLS

PRAY KNOW REWARD

THANKS TALKS COVERS

REMEMBER

```
T Y T H A N K S M P
X T Y S H G Z G N K
D S V V L U X C K N
R N T Q V L N B W O
A I T M J S A G R W
W A P H R T N F R Y
E G R E A M T Y A Y
R A V L N L M R N B
M O K K C G P N L R
C S R E B M E M E R
```

PUZZLE 14

What does the Bible say about being lazy?

1

Do not be lazy but always work hard. Work for the Lord with a heart full of love for Him.
ROMANS 12:11

2

Anyone who steals must stop it! He must work with his hands so he will have what he needs and can give to those who need help.
EPHESIANS 4:28

3

The soul of the lazy person has strong desires but gets nothing, but the soul of the one who does his best gets more than he needs.
PROVERBS 13:4

4

He who works his land will have more than enough food, but he who wastes his time will become very poor.
PROVERBS 28:19

5

Do not love sleep, or you will become poor. Open your eyes, and you will be filled with food.
PROVERBS 20:13

6

The path of the lazy man is grown over with thorns, but the path of the faithful is a good road.
PROVERBS 15:19

7

Anyone who does not take care of his family and those in his house has turned away from the faith. He is worse than a person who has never put his trust in Christ.
1 TIMOTHY 5:8

8

Keep away from any Christian who is lazy and who does not do what we taught you.
2 THESSALONIANS 3:6

9

When we were with you, we told you that if a man does not work, he should not eat.
2 THESSALONIANS 3:10

10

Go to the ant, O lazy person. Watch and think about her ways, and be wise.
PROVERBS 6:6

Find These Words in the Puzzle!

HARD   WORKS   LAZY
HANDS   SLEEP   EAT
DESIRES   THORNS   WISE
            FAMILY

L T T L F D M T T V
Y L I M A F N W A J
W J H D E S I R E S
D M K J R T Y W B G
R K G F H W H Z R R
A P M O S Q O Q A S
H C R E L G Y R D L
C N S B E K L N K T
S I M T E N A C W S
W V M H P H R V X J

1

The few things that the man right with God has is **better** than the riches of many sinful men.
PSALM 37:16

2

Tell those who are rich in this world not to be proud and not to trust in their money. Money cannot be **trusted**.
1 TIMOTHY 6:17

3

"Both riches and honor come from You. You **rule** over all."
1 CHRONICLES 29:12

4

He who trusts in his riches will fall, but those who are right with God will **grow** like a green leaf.
PROVERBS 11:28

5

Riches are of no use in the day of God's **anger**, but being right with God saves from death.
PROVERBS 11:4

6

He who loves money will never have **enough** money to make him happy. It is the same for the one who loves to get many things.
ECCLESIASTES 5:10

7

We came into this world with nothing. For sure, when we **die**, we will take nothing with us.
1 TIMOTHY 6:7

8

Keep your lives free from the love of **money**. Be happy with what you have. God has said, "I will never leave you or let you be alone."
HEBREWS 13:5

9

"You cannot have both God and riches as your **boss** at the same time."
MATTHEW 6:24

10

The love of money is the beginning of all kinds of **sin**. Some people have turned from the faith because of their love for money.
1 TIMOTHY 6:10

Find These Words in the Puzzle!

BETTER
TRUSTED
RULE

GROW
ANGER
ENOUGH
DIE

MONEY
BOSS
SIN

X G N H D D M Z T A
V S R V R U L E V N
T S Z F M X R T I G
L O F V B B E S D E
D B Y B L N T E B R
Q J T E O M T R G T
R Y G U N S E E I D
Y K G R U O B T G R
Z H N R O C M J D N
M T T L R W G K H K

PUZZLE 16

What does the Bible say about prayer?

1

"Ask, and what you are asking for will be given to you. Look, and what you are looking for you will find. *Knock*, and the door you are knocking on will be opened to you."

MATTHEW 7:7

2

"All things you ask for in prayer, you will receive if you have *faith*."

MATTHEW 21:22

3

"And it will be before they call, I will answer. While they are still *speaking*, I will hear."

ISAIAH 65:24

4

Tell your sins to each other. And pray for each other so you may be *healed*. The prayer from the heart of a man right with God has much power.

JAMES 5:16

5

"When you pray, go into a *room* by yourself. After you have shut the door, pray to your Father Who is in secret. Then your Father Who sees in secret will reward you."

MATTHEW 6:6

6

The Lord is far from the sinful, but He hears the *prayer* of those who are right with Him.

PROVERBS 15:29

7

"You are bad and you know how to give good things to your *children*. How much more will your Father in heaven give good things to those who ask Him?"

MATTHEW 7:11

8

"Whatever you ask for when you pray, have faith that you will *receive* it. Then you will get it."

MARK 11:24

9

You must pray at all times as the Holy Spirit *leads* you to pray.

EPHESIANS 6:18

10

Is anyone among you *suffering*? He should pray. Is anyone happy? He should sing songs of thanks to God.

JAMES 5:13

Find These Words in the Puzzle!

KNOCK   HEALED   RECEIVE
FAITH   ROOM   LEADS
SPEAKING   PRAYER   SUFFERING
             CHILDREN

Z T E M R P R Y V N
L G N V R X O M K G
N M R A I Z O S C N
V X Y H H E M D O I
Z E Z T E B C A N R
R W I Q T A L E K E
V A F Q R B L L R F
F X H N V V P E F F
S P E A K I N G D U
C N E R D L I H C S

PUZZLE 17

What does the Bible say about being saved?

1

Jesus said to him, "For sure, I tell you, unless a man is born again, he cannot see the holy nation of God."

JOHN 3:3

2

He wants all people to be saved from the punishment of sin. He wants them to come to know the truth.

1 TIMOTHY 2:4

3

When you were dead in your sins, you were not set free from the sinful things of the world. But God forgave your sins and gave you new life through Christ.

COLOSSIANS 2:13

4

"There is no other name under heaven given to men by which we can be saved."

ACTS 4:12

5

Our hope is in the living God, the One Who would save all men. He saves those who believe in Him.

1 TIMOTHY 4:10

6

God, the One Who saves, showed how kind He was and how He loved us by saving us from the punishment of sin.

TITUS 3:4–5

7

If you say with your mouth that Jesus is Lord, and believe in your heart that God raised Him from the dead, you will be saved from the punishment of sin.

ROMANS 10:9

8

"I tell you, anyone who hears My Word and puts his trust in Him Who sent Me has life that lasts forever."

JOHN 5:24

9

By His loving-favor you have been saved from the punishment of sin through faith. It is not by anything you have done. It is a gift of God.

EPHESIANS 2:8

10

I am not ashamed of the Good News. It is the power of God. It is the way He saves men from the punishment of their sins if they put their trust in Him.

ROMANS 1:16

Find These Words in the Puzzle!

AGAIN   HEAVEN   FOREVER
PUNISHMENT   BELIEVE   GIFT
DEAD   KIND   POWER
               RAISED

H	B	D	E	S	I	A	R	W	T
L	E	D	Q	P	F	L	Q	N	R
R	L	A	H	P	K	M	E	I	L
E	I	M	V	I	R	M	N	A	C
V	E	N	N	E	H	M	N	G	G
E	V	D	W	S	N	T	V	A	G
R	E	O	I	X	L	T	F	F	W
O	P	N	L	D	E	A	D	I	W
F	U	R	R	R	H	L	L	T	G
P	N	J	N	Y	W	Q	M	R	H

PUZZLE 18

What does the Bible say about being wise?

1

If you do not have wisdom, ask God for it. He is always ready to give it to you and will never say you are wrong for asking.

JAMES 1:5

2

For God has given wisdom and much learning and joy to the person who is good in God's eyes.

ECCLESIASTES 2:26

3

For the Lord gives wisdom. Much learning and understanding come from His mouth.

PROVERBS 2:6

4

You want truth deep within the heart. And You will make me know wisdom in the hidden part.

PSALM 51:6

5

Sinful men do not understand what is right and fair, but those who look to the Lord understand all things.

PROVERBS 28:5

6

To get wisdom is much better than getting gold. To get understanding should be chosen instead of silver.

PROVERBS 16:16

7

Do not fool yourself. If anyone thinks he knows a lot about the things of this world, he had better become a fool. Then he may become wise.

1 CORINTHIANS 3:18

8

"Whoever hears these words of Mine and does them, will be like a wise man who built his house on rock."

MATTHEW 7:24

9

Teach us to understand how many days we have. Then we will have a heart of wisdom to give You.

PSALM 90:12

10

The fear of the Lord is the teaching for wisdom, and having no pride comes before honor.

PROVERBS 15:33

Find These Words in the Puzzle!

READY
LEARNING
MOUTH

HIDDEN
FAIR
WISDOM
FOOL

ROCK
UNDERSTAND
TEACHING

D K Y N L O O F G J
N Z C Q H L R N K M
A J N O C I I L X F
T L Y K R N D F M A
S P D R R F W D X I
R K A A F I Q H E R
E Y E W S M F L G N
D L R D Y V J P N N
N D O N X M O U T H
U M G N I H C A E T

PUZZLE 19

What does the Bible say about the devil?

1

The devil has sinned from the beginning. But the Son of God came to destroy the works of the devil.

1 JOHN 3:8

2

"It is expected of the devil to lie, for he is a liar and the father of lies."

JOHN 8:44

3

"The robber comes only to steal and to kill and to destroy."

JOHN 10:10

4

So give yourselves to God. Stand against the devil and he will run away from you.

JAMES 4:7

5

God, Who is our peace, will soon crush Satan under your feet.

ROMANS 16:20

6

The devil is working against you. He is walking around like a hungry lion with his mouth open. He is looking for someone to eat.

1 PETER 5:8

7

Our fight is not with people. It is against the leaders and the powers and the spirits of darkness in this world.

EPHESIANS 6:12

8

It is no surprise! The devil makes himself look like an angel of light.

2 CORINTHIANS 11:14

9

Jesus said to them, "I saw Satan fall from heaven like lightning."

LUKE 10:18

10

We know that we belong to God, but the whole world is under the power of the devil.

1 JOHN 5:19

Find These Words in the Puzzle!

SINNED	RUN	ANGEL
LIAR	CRUSH	LIGHTNING
ROBBER	LION	WORLD
	DARKNESS	

```
F  S  S  E  N  K  R  A  D  L  L
D  G  F  Q  K  Y  Q  M  I  Y
E  N  C  B  G  X  Y  O  F  R
N  I  R  W  V  P  N  N  K  T
N  N  U  R  O  B  B  E  R  J
I  T  S  L  C  G  Q  W  D  K
S  H  H  Z  E  G  T  L  Y  R
D  G  R  R  D  G  R  X  A  F
P  I  F  M  U  O  N  I  T  K
L  L  J  N  W  N  L  A  T  V
```

PUZZLE 20

What does the Bible say about angels?

1

Are not all the angels spirits who work for God? They are sent out to help those who are to be saved from the punishment of sin.

HEBREWS 1:14

2

He will tell His angels to care for you and keep you in all your ways.

PSALM 91:11

3

"After people are raised from the dead, they do not marry. They are like the angels in heaven."

MATTHEW 22:30

4

Praise the Lord, you powerful angels of His who do what He says, obeying His voice as He speaks!

PSALM 103:20

5

The angel of the Lord stays close around those who fear Him, and He takes them out of trouble.

PSALM 34:7

6

"He will send His angels with the loud sound of a horn. They will gather God's people together from the four winds."

MATTHEW 24:31

7

When God brought His first-born Son, Jesus, into the world, He said, "Let all the angels of God worship Him."

HEBREWS 1:6

8

Do not forget to be kind to strangers and let them stay in your home. Some people have had angels in their homes without knowing it.

HEBREWS 13:2

9

The angel said to them, "Do not be afraid. See! I bring you good news of great joy which is for all people."

LUKE 2:10

10

"Do you not think that I can pray to My Father? At once He would send Me more than 70,000 angels."

MATTHEW 26:53

Find These Words in the Puzzle!

SPIRITS
CARE
HEAVEN

POWERFUL
CLOSE
HORN
WORSHIP

STRANGERS
NEWS
FATHER

F S C A R E W L B R
A R P I H S R O W C
T E P W S N G K T L
H G S O K W N T N O
E N T K W V E E B S
R A I W H E V N W E
W R R L Y A R H K Q
H T I D E M O F Q J
N S P H W R M Z U L
H N S T N D K T F L

PUZZLE 21

What does the Bible say about God's Word?

1

The opening up of Your Word gives light. It gives understanding to the child-like.

PSALM 119:130

2

Your Word is a lamp to my feet and a light to my path.

PSALM 119:105

3

So then, faith comes to us by hearing the Good News. And the Good News comes by someone preaching it.

ROMANS 10:17

4

As new babies want milk, you should want to drink the pure milk which is God's Word so you will grow up and be saved from the punishment of sin.

1 PETER 2:2

5

"Keep these words of mine in your heart and in your soul."

DEUTERONOMY 11:18

6

All the Holy Writings are God-given and are made alive by Him. Man is helped when he is taught God's Word.

2 TIMOTHY 3:16

7

Obey the Word of God. If you hear only and do not act, you are only fooling yourself.

JAMES 1:22

8

"Heaven and earth will pass away, but My words will not pass away."

MATTHEW 24:35

9

Jesus said, "It is written, 'Man is not to live on bread only. Man is to live by every word that God speaks.'"

MATTHEW 4:4

10

The Word (Christ) was in the beginning. The Word was with God. The Word was God.

JOHN 1:1

Find These Words in the Puzzle!

LIGHT	MILK	PASS
LAMP	KEEP	BREAD
HEARING	HOLY	BEGINNING
	ACT	

G V H H E A R I N G
N K Q T K T X M P D
I E J H S T W M B A
N E M G T S A P H E
N P K I N L A O J R
I B F L R R L P P B
G J M K N Y N J T C
E H K I M P Z K B G
B T L M L K M T W N
N J L P N K M T C A

PUZZLE 22

What does the Bible say about worshiping God?

1

Come, let us bow down in worship. Let us get down on our knees before the Lord Who made us.
PSALM 95:6

2

"God is Spirit. Those who worship Him must worship Him in spirit and in truth."
JOHN 4:24

3

Let everything that has breath praise the Lord. Praise the Lord!
PSALM 150:6

4

The Lord is great and our praise to Him should be great. He is too great for anyone to understand.
PSALM 145:3

5

Be lifted up high above the heavens, O God. Let Your shining-greatness be over all the earth.
PSALM 108:5

6

Sing praises to the Lord, for He has done great things. Let this be known in all the earth.
ISAIAH 12:5

7

Worship the Lord in holy clothing. May all the earth shake in fear before Him.
PSALM 96:9

8

Let your bodies be a living and holy gift given to God. He is pleased with this kind of gift. This is the true worship that you should give Him.
ROMANS 12:1

9

Jesus said to the devil, "Get behind Me, Satan! For it is written, 'You must worship the Lord your God. You must obey Him only.'"
LUKE 4:8

10

Since we have received a holy nation that cannot be moved, let us be thankful. Let us please God and worship Him with honor and fear.
HEBREWS 12:28

Find These Words in the Puzzle!

BOW   GREAT   BODIES
TRUTH   ABOVE   LORD
PRAISE   SING   HONOR
                SHAKE

```
S E K A H S N L D D
K E N X H X H D R Q
B M I T R G V Z O Z
K L U D R H R H L J
H R L O O R Z E Q T
T L N S D B T A A T
F O I Y J B W B W T
H N C R N Q O O J C
G N H N T M B V R J
R N P R A I S E D D
```

PUZZLE 23

What does the Bible say about faith?

1

Now faith is being sure we will get what we hope for. It is being sure of what we cannot see.
HEBREWS 11:1

2

Jesus said to him. . ."The one who has faith can do all things."
MARK 9:23

3

Jesus said to him, "Thomas, because you have seen Me, you believe. Those are happy who have never seen Me and yet believe!"
JOHN 20:29

4

Our life is lived by faith. We do not live by what we see in front of us.
2 CORINTHIANS 5:7

5

Every child of God has power over the sins of the world. The way we have power over the sins of the world is by our faith.
1 JOHN 5:4

6

Jesus said, "Go! Your faith has healed you." At once he could see and he followed Jesus down the road.
MARK 10:52

7

When we believe in our hearts, we are made right with God. We tell with our mouth how we were saved from the punishment of sin.
ROMANS 10:10

8

A faith that does not do things is a dead faith.
JAMES 2:17

9

Now that we have been made right with God by putting our trust in Him, we have peace with Him. It is because of what our Lord Jesus Christ did for us.
ROMANS 5:1

10

You must have faith as you ask Him. You must not doubt. Anyone who doubts is like a wave which is pushed around by the sea.
JAMES 1:6

Find These Words in the Puzzle!

SURE	SEE	DEAD
JESUS	CHILD	RIGHT
THOMAS	HEALED	DOUBT
	BELIEVE	

```
L N K N L B D K H Q
Y H N K D P G A H R
T T H O M A S E E J
C B X Q K R A T S D
H T N M T L B U F T
I H E X E U S H R H
L G R D O E S K G G
D I U D J R M E L F
Z R S F B R H B E L
K B E V E I L E B T
```

PUZZLE 24

What does the Bible say about the Holy Spirit?

1

"I will ask My Father and He will give you another Helper. He will be with you forever. He is the Spirit of Truth."

JOHN 14:16–17

2

"The Holy Spirit is coming. He will lead you into all truth."

JOHN 16:13

3

"I will put My Spirit within you and cause you to follow My Laws and be careful to do what I tell you."

EZEKIEL 36:27

4

Christ gave you the Holy Spirit and He lives in you. You do not need anyone to teach you. The Holy Spirit is able to teach you all things.

1 JOHN 2:27

5

We have not received the spirit of the world. God has given us His Holy Spirit that we may know about the things given to us by Him.

1 CORINTHIANS 2:12

6

Do you not know that your body is a house of God where the Holy Spirit lives? God gave you His Holy Spirit. Now you belong to God. You do not belong to yourselves.

1 CORINTHIANS 6:19

7

Do not make God's Holy Spirit have sorrow for the way you live. The Holy Spirit has put a mark on you for the day you will be set free.

EPHESIANS 4:30

8

"We have seen these things and are telling about them. The Holy Spirit makes these things known also. God gives His Spirit to those who obey Him."

ACTS 5:32

9

When Paul laid his hands on them, the Holy Spirit came on them. They started to talk in special sounds and to speak God's Word.

ACTS 19:6

10

No part of the Holy Writings came long ago because of what man wanted to write. But holy men who belonged to God spoke what the Holy Spirit told them.

2 PETER 1:21

Find These Words in the Puzzle!

HELPER   LIVES   OBEY
LEAD   GOD   SPEAK
WITHIN   BELONG   HOLY
                SORROW

```
W  O  R  R  O  S  K  R  B  N
W  I  T  H  I  N  Z  E  M  Q
M  C  R  N  Y  N  L  P  J  H
V  Q  F  L  G  O  D  L  T  M
K  Y  O  L  N  K  D  E  R  R
M  H  K  G  I  A  Y  H  N  W
G  G  A  W  E  V  T  E  M  M
O  N  E  L  H  H  E  Q  B  P
D  X  P  T  T  B  L  S  R  O
T  T  S  C  G  M  R  L  R  R
```

PUZZLE 25

What does the Bible say about being patient?

1

Do not let yourselves get tired of doing good. If we do not give up, we will get what is coming to us at the right time.
GALATIANS 6:9

2

"The one who stays true to the end will be saved."
MATTHEW 24:13

3

You must be willing to wait without giving up. After you have done what God wants you to do, God will give you what He promised you.
HEBREWS 10:36

4

My Christian brothers, you should be happy when you have all kinds of tests. You know these prove your faith. It helps you not to give up.
JAMES 1:2–3

5

He who is slow to get angry has great understanding, but he who has a quick temper makes his foolish way look right.
PROVERBS 14:29

6

But if we hope for something we do not yet see, we must learn how to wait for it.
ROMANS 8:25

7

Wait for the Lord. Be strong. Let your heart be strong. Yes, wait for the Lord.
PSALM 27:14

8

"The Lord will fight for you. All you have to do is keep still."
EXODUS 14:14

9

Christian brothers, be willing to wait for the Lord to come again. Learn from the farmer. He waits for the good fruit from the earth until the early and late rains come.
JAMES 5:7

10

Love does not give up.
1 CORINTHIANS 13:4

Find These Words in the Puzzle!

TIRED   TESTS   STILL

SAVED   SLOW   FARMER

WAIT   HOPE   LOVE

                 STRONG

```
G  W  A  I  T  M  N  L  R  F
G  G  K  R  E  N  D  Z  E  F
B  L  L  V  L  E  N  L  M  T
C  D  O  V  V  L  H  H  R  W
T  L  R  A  P  O  I  L  A  S
G  E  S  X  P  D  R  T  F  L
F  W  S  E  X  E  N  B  S  O
F  T  Z  T  J  R  N  L  R  W
G  D  Q  P  S  I  B  G  K  L
N  G  N  O  R  T  S  F  V  B
```

PUZZLE 26

What does the Bible say about feeling lonely?

1

"I will not leave you without help as children without parents. I will come to you."

JOHN 14:18

2

"I will be a Father to you. You will be My sons and daughters, says the All-powerful God."

2 CORINTHIANS 6:18

3

"See, I am with you. I will care for you everywhere you go."

GENESIS 28:15

4

When you have Christ, you are complete.

COLOSSIANS 2:10

5

Because I suffer and am in need, let the Lord think of me. You are my help and the One Who sets me free.

PSALM 40:17

6

Turn to me and show me Your loving-kindness. For I am alone and in trouble.

PSALM 25:16

7

"I am with you always, even to the end of the world."

MATTHEW 28:20

8

Yes, even if I walk through the valley of the shadow of death, I will not be afraid of anything, because You are with me.

PSALM 23:4

9

God in His holy house is a father to those who have no father. And He keeps the women safe whose husbands have died.

PSALM 68:5

10

Everyone left me. I hope this will not be held against them. But the Lord was with me.

2 TIMOTHY 4:16–17

Find These Words in the Puzzle!

CHILDREN
FATHER
EVERYWHERE

COMPLETE
FREE
ALONE
ALWAYS

VALLEY
SAFE
EVERYONE

```
E  E  V  E  R  Y  W  H  E  R  E
E  C  Y  N  W  H  L  J  P  A
V  O  R  E  S  Y  A  W  L  A
E  M  E  R  Y  M  T  O  Q  Q
R  P  F  D  H  E  N  W  R  D
Y  L  A  L  F  E  L  E  G  M
O  E  S  I  F  R  H  L  K  K
N  T  T  H  K  T  E  H  A  P
E  E  F  C  A  K  Q  E  L  V
T  N  T  F  J  N  T  Q  P  R
```

PUZZLE 27

What does the Bible say about sin?

1

You get what is coming to you when you sin. It is death! But God's free gift is life that lasts forever. It is given to us by our Lord Jesus Christ.
ROMANS 6:23

2

For all men have sinned and have missed the shining-greatness of God.
ROMANS 3:23

3

If we say that we have no sin, we lie to ourselves and the truth is not in us.
1 JOHN 1:8

4

The person who keeps on sinning is guilty of not obeying the Law of God. For sin is breaking the Law of God.
1 JOHN 3:4

5

Jesus answered them, "For sure, I tell you, everyone who sins is the servant of sin because sin has a hold on him."
JOHN 8:34

6

If you know what is right to do but you do not do it, you sin.
JAMES 4:17

7

When he does what his bad thoughts tell him to do, he sins. When sin completes its work, it brings death.
JAMES 1:15

8

If we keep on sinning because we want to after we have received and know the truth, there is no gift that will take away sins then.
HEBREWS 10:26

9

He carried our sins in His own body when He died on a cross. In doing this, we may be dead to sin and alive to all that is right and good.
1 PETER 2:24

10

"Whatever comes out of a man is what makes the man sinful."
MARK 7:20

Find These Words in the Puzzle!

DEATH GUILTY SINNING
MISSED SERVANT ALIVE
LIE KNOW OUT
COMPLETES

```
Z  H  G  S  R  B  N  C  Y  M
P  S  L  E  E  L  I  E  M  D
M  E  L  R  R  V  T  R  E  Z
N  T  W  V  G  D  I  S  P  K
L  E  Q  A  F  U  S  L  N  K
K  L  H  N  K  I  I  O  A  T
F  P  T  T  M  D  W  L  U  G
D  M  A  X  J  R  L  O  T  G
P  O  E  J  L  W  M  L  H  Y
J  C  D  G  N  I  N  N  I  S
```

PUZZLE 28

What does the Bible say about miracles?

1

Jesus looked at them and said, "This cannot be done by men but God can do anything."
MARK 10:27

2

You made the parts inside me. You put me together inside my mother. I will give thanks to You, for the greatness of the way I was made brings fear.
PSALM 139:13–14

3

"It is faith in Christ that has made this man well and strong."
ACTS 3:16

4

God used Paul to do powerful special works.
ACTS 19:11

5

"I am the Lord, the God of all flesh. Is anything too hard for Me?"
JEREMIAH 32:27

6

God proved what they said was true by showing us special things to see and by doing powerful works.
HEBREWS 2:4

7

Jesus did many other powerful works in front of His followers. They are not written in this book.
JOHN 20:30

8

"For sure, I tell you, whoever puts his trust in Me can do the things I am doing. He will do even greater things than these because I am going to the Father."
JOHN 14:12

9

When the demon was put out of him, the man was able to talk. Many people were surprised and wondered about it.
MATTHEW 9:33

10

"He does great things, too great for us to understand. He does too many wonderful things for us to number."
JOB 5:9

Find These Words in the Puzzle!

GOD
GREATNESS
WELL

POWERFUL
HARD
SPECIAL
JESUS

TRUST
SURPRISED
WONDERFUL

Y L U F R E D N O W
P D E S I R P R U S
C O S U S E J B S R
T T W E L L W E G S
D S N E T X N Z P H
O L U N R T D E N A
G N M R A F C L G R
K C M E T I U Y D D
B T R B A F B L H T
Q G N L Q Y L P G W

PUZZLE 29

What does the Bible say about being sick?

1

Is anyone among you sick? He should send for the church leaders and they should pray for him. They should pour oil on him in the name of the Lord.

JAMES 5:14

2

Jesus went over all Galilee. . . . He healed all kinds of sickness and disease among the people.

MATTHEW 4:23

3

The Lord will give him strength on his bed of sickness. When he is sick, You will make him well again.

PSALM 41:3

4

Jesus called His twelve followers to Him. He gave them power to put out demons and to heal all kinds of sickness and disease.

MATTHEW 10:1

5

It happened as the early preacher Isaiah said it would happen. He said, "He took on Himself our sickness and carried away our diseases."

MATTHEW 8:17

6

Be kind to me, O Lord, for I am weak. O Lord, heal me for my bones are shaken.

PSALM 6:2

7

The sisters sent word to Jesus, saying, "Lord, your friend is sick!" When Jesus heard this, He said, "This sickness will not end in death. It has happened so that it will bring honor to God."

JOHN 11:3–4

8

Hope that is put off makes the heart sick, but a desire that comes into being is a tree of life.

PROVERBS 13:12

9

The father of Publius was sick with a stomach sickness. Paul went to see him. He prayed and laid his hands on him and the man was healed.

ACTS 28:8

10

"God will take away all their tears. There will be no more death or sorrow or crying or pain. All the old things have passed away."

REVELATION 21:4

Find These Words in the Puzzle!

CHURCH   DISEASE   DESIRE
HEALED   ISAIAH   HANDS
STRENGTH   WEAK   PASSED
            HONOR

E J D W Y G M L L D
K R E I V K L V E Z
L A I K S W L L D D
K X S S R E A Q E X
I H D D E E A S T K
S C N B H D S S M K
A R A T T A X R E J
I U H W P R O N O H
A H S T R E N G T H
H C Y F C T Q X K R

PUZZLE 30

What does the Bible say about getting along with others?

1

It is better to live in a desert land than with a woman who argues and causes trouble.
PROVERBS 21:19

2

Do not let what is good for you be talked about as bad.
ROMANS 14:16

3

Be at peace with all men. Live a holy life. No one will see the Lord without having that kind of life.
HEBREWS 12:14

4

The beginning of trouble is like letting out water. So stop arguing before fighting breaks out.
PROVERBS 17:14

5

Live and work without pride. Be gentle and kind. Do not be hard on others. Let love keep you from doing that.
EPHESIANS 4:2

6

So comfort each other and make each other strong as you are already doing.
1 THESSALONIANS 5:11

7

"Those who make peace are happy, because they will be called the sons of God."
MATTHEW 5:9

8

Be gentle when you try to teach those who are against what you say. God may change their hearts so they will turn to the truth.
2 TIMOTHY 2:25

9

Let us not become proud in ways in which we should not. We must not make hard feelings among ourselves as Christians.
GALATIANS 5:26

10

As much as you can, live in peace with all men.
ROMANS 12:18

Find These Words in the Puzzle!

ARGUES
GOOD
HOLY

FIGHTING
GENTLE
COMFORT
GOD

TEACH
FEELINGS
PEACE

F	V	T	H	D	B	N	G	N	H
I	K	B	Y	C	K	E	S	S	C
G	J	D	V	V	N	E	Z	G	A
H	T	G	O	T	U	C	K	N	E
T	F	M	L	G	Y	A	W	I	T
I	G	E	R	K	J	E	C	L	W
N	T	A	G	R	H	P	B	E	K
G	K	J	J	G	Y	O	Y	E	X
R	H	V	G	O	O	D	L	F	N
T	R	O	F	M	O	C	F	Y	P

PUZZLE 31

What does the Bible say about God's blessings?

1

Whatever is good and perfect comes to us from God.

JAMES 1:17

2

"His sun shines on bad people and on good people. He sends rain on those who are right with God and on those who are not right with God."

MATTHEW 5:45

3

The good that comes from the Lord makes one rich, and He adds no sorrow to it.

PROVERBS 10:22

4

God can give you all you need. He will give you more than enough. You will have everything you need for yourselves. And you will have enough left over to give when there is a need.

2 CORINTHIANS 9:8

5

Happy is the nation whose God is the Lord. Happy are the people He has chosen for His own.

PSALM 33:12

6

Let us honor and thank the God and Father of our Lord Jesus Christ. He has already given us a taste of what heaven is like.

EPHESIANS 1:3

7

"God has raised up His Son Jesus and has sent Him to you first to give God's favor to each of you who will turn away from his sinful ways."

ACTS 3:26

8

"May the Lord bring good to you and keep you. May the Lord make His face shine upon you, and be kind to you."

NUMBERS 6:24–25

9

From Him Who has so much we have all received loving-favor, one loving-favor after another.

JOHN 1:16

10

"The Lord will send good upon you in your store-houses and in all your work. He will bring good to you in the land the Lord your God gives you."

DEUTERONOMY 28:8

Find These Words in the Puzzle!

PERFECT   ENOUGH   FACE

SHINES   HAPPY   RECEIVED

RICH   TASTE   LAND

                     FAVOR

```
N  L  D  W  K  R  I  C  H  D
L  W  E  K  V  B  F  K  L  D
T  T  V  F  K  T  P  T  N  S
W  C  I  E  W  M  Y  A  E  H
H  E  E  P  N  J  L  N  T  T
A  F  C  C  F  O  I  L  A  H
P  R  E  H  A  H  U  S  G  R
P  E  R  P  S  F  T  G  Q  N
Y  P  F  Z  P  E  G  M  H  D
G  Q  Q  R  Y  R  O  V  A  F
```

PUZZLE 32

What does the Bible say about stealing?

1

"Do not steal."
EXODUS 20:15

2

Those who steal. . .or take things that are not theirs, will have no place in the holy nation of God.
1 CORINTHIANS 6:10

3

"If the robber is caught he will pay twice as much as the loss."
EXODUS 22:7

4

"Do not make it hard for your neighbor or rob him. You should not keep the pay of a man who works for you until the next morning."
LEVITICUS 19:13

5

Riches taken by wrong-doing do no good, but doing what is right and good saves from death.
PROVERBS 10:2

6

Do not get money in a wrong way or be proud in stolen things. If you get more riches, do not set your heart on them.
PSALM 62:10

7

"Will a man rob God? Yet you are robbing Me! But you say, 'How have we robbed You?' You have not given Me the tenth part of what you receive and your gifts."
MALACHI 3:8

8

"For I, the Lord, love what is right and fair. I hate stealing and what is wrong."
ISAIAH 61:8

9

Bread a man gets by lying is sweet to him, but later his mouth will be filled with sand.
PROVERBS 20:17

10

"Do not lie about the weight or price of anything."
LEVITICUS 19:35

Find These Words in the Puzzle!

STEAL

THEIRS

TWICE

NEIGHBOR

TAKEN

WRONG

ROBBING

FAIR

SAND

WEIGHT

```
P  N  M  G  C  H  P  T  V  Q
K  L  T  G  N  I  B  B  O  R
N  A  B  M  N  J  G  Z  K  S
D  E  N  T  W  I  C  E  R  N
N  T  I  R  R  N  M  I  L  T
A  S  O  G  T  I  E  M  H  A
S  N  L  N  H  H  A  G  Q  K
G  Y  F  X  T  B  I  F  D  E
V  H  R  R  H  E  O  N  N  N
M  Z  L  T  W  R  K  R  N  Z
```

PUZZLE 33

What does the Bible say about time to come?

1

"For I know the *plans* I have for you," says the Lord, "plans for well-being and not for trouble, to give you a future and a hope."
JEREMIAH 29:11

2

There are many plans in a man's *heart*, but it is the Lord's plan that will stand.
PROVERBS 19:21

3

The Lord has made all things for His own plans, even the sinful for the day of *trouble*.
PROVERBS 16:4

4

You do not know about *tomorrow*. What is your life? It is like fog. You see it and soon it is gone.
JAMES 4:14

5

The heaven we see now and the earth we live on now have been kept by His word. They will be kept until they are to be *destroyed* by fire.
2 PETER 3:7

6

Do not talk much about tomorrow, for you do not *know* what a day will bring.
PROVERBS 27:1

7

"I tell from the *beginning* what will happen in the end."
ISAIAH 46:10

8

"There is hope for your future," says the Lord, "and your children will *return* to their own land."
JEREMIAH 31:17

9

You must be willing to wait also. Be strong in your hearts because the Lord is coming again *soon*.
JAMES 5:8

10

Do not let your heart be jealous of sinners, but *live* in the fear of the Lord always. For sure there is a future and your hope will not be cut off.
PROVERBS 23:17–18

Find These Words in the Puzzle!

PLANS   TOMORROW   RETURN
HEART   DESTROYED   SOON
TROUBLE   KNOW   LIVE
               BEGINNING

R S T N R U T E R G
D N H O V V T R N L
E A V F M R Y I Q V
S L T K A O N R T E
T P R E L N R F M V
R N H Z I K F R K I
O N O G N T T Y O L
Y C E O G G T M B W
E B W C S T M V N V
D X B T R O U B L E

PUZZLE 34

What does the Bible say about God's power?

1

He knows the number of the stars. He gives names to all of them. Great is our Lord, and great in power. His understanding has no end.

PSALM 147:4–5

2

Jesus came and said to them, "All power has been given to Me in heaven and on earth."

MATTHEW 28:18

3

O Lord, Your right hand is great in power. O Lord, Your right hand destroys those who hate You.

EXODUS 15:6

4

O Lord, You have great power, shining-greatness and strength. Yes, everything in heaven and on earth belongs to You.

1 CHRONICLES 29:11

5

"The pillars of heaven shake with fear. They are surprised and afraid of His sharp words. He made the sea quiet by His power."

JOB 26:11–12

6

It is He Who made the earth by His power, and the world by His wisdom.

JEREMIAH 10:12

7

From the beginning of the world, men could see what God is like through the things He has made. This shows His power that lasts forever.

ROMANS 1:20

8

Preaching about the cross sounds foolish to those who are dying in sin. But it is the power of God to those of us who are being saved.

1 CORINTHIANS 1:18

9

God is able to do much more than we ask or think through His power working in us.

EPHESIANS 3:20

10

"All-powerful Lord God, the One Who is and Who was and Who is to come, we thank You because You are using Your great power and have become Leader."

REVELATION 11:17

Find These Words in the Puzzle!

GREAT   HEAVEN   SAVED
POWER   SHAKE   WORKING
LORD   WISDOM   LEADER
      FOREVER

```
H V S R D L M W D G
X E H K R E I X N N
F Y A T L S V H Y I
N H K V D R D A R K
F M E O E L J E S R
R L M W W N D M T O
J L O R D A L J A W
K P T K E Q R P E M
Y C F L L F K K R P
R E V E R O F R G T
```

PUZZLE 35

What does the Bible say about God's wisdom?

1

"As the heavens are higher than the earth, so are My ways higher than your ways, and My thoughts than your thoughts."
ISAIAH 55:9

2

God's plan looked foolish to men, but it is wiser than the best plans of men.
1 CORINTHIANS 1:25

3

God's riches are so great! The things He knows and His wisdom are so deep! No one can understand His thoughts.
ROMANS 11:33

4

In Christ are hidden all the riches of wisdom and understanding.
COLOSSIANS 2:3

5

Christ is the power and wisdom of God to those who are chosen to be saved from the punishment of sin for both Jews and Greeks.
1 CORINTHIANS 1:24

6

"Let the name of God be honored forever and ever, for wisdom and power belong to Him."
DANIEL 2:20

7

"With God are wisdom and strength. Wise words and understanding belong to Him."
JOB 12:13

8

We speak about these things also. We do not use words of man's wisdom. We use words given to us by the Holy Spirit.
1 CORINTHIANS 2:13

9

The Holy Writings say, "I will destroy the wisdom of the wise people. I will put aside the learning of those who think they know a lot."
1 CORINTHIANS 1:19

10

May God, Who only is wise, be honored forever through our Lord Jesus Christ.
ROMANS 16:27

Find These Words in the Puzzle

HIGHER
WISER
UNDERSTAND

HIDDEN
CHOSEN
BELONG
WORDS

SPIRIT
LEARNING
HONORED

L	R	G	N	I	N	R	A	E	L
U	N	D	E	R	S	T	A	N	D
D	R	T	I	R	I	P	S	N	W
M	E	D	C	C	X	H	L	O	L
H	H	R	H	H	R	Y	R	T	R
N	G	V	O	M	I	D	G	E	L
M	I	T	S	N	S	D	S	L	P
B	H	D	E	K	O	I	D	T	H
T	L	W	N	M	W	H	R	E	M
C	B	E	L	O	N	G	L	K	N

PUZZLE 36

What does the Bible say about God's love?

1

"For God so loved the world that He gave His only Son. Whoever puts his trust in God's Son will not be lost but will have life that lasts forever."

JOHN 3:16

2

God showed His love to us. While we were still sinners, Christ died for us.

ROMANS 5:8

3

We have come to know and believe the love God has for us. God is love.

1 JOHN 4:16

4

"The mountains may be taken away and the hills may shake, but My loving-kindness will not be taken from you."

ISAIAH 54:10

5

Give thanks to the God of heaven, for His loving-kindness lasts forever.

PSALM 136:26

6

But You, O Lord, are a God full of love and pity. You are slow to anger and rich in loving-kindness and truth.

PSALM 86:15

7

See what great love the Father has for us that He would call us His children.

1 JOHN 3:1

8

"No one can have greater love than to give his life for his friends."

JOHN 15:13

9

Of what great worth is Your loving-kindness, O God! The children of men come and are safe in the shadow of Your wings.

PSALM 36:7

10

We love Him because He loved us first.

1 JOHN 4:19

Find These Words in the Puzzle!

WORLD
DIED
BELIEVE

MOUNTAINS
THANKS
PITY
FATHER

FRIENDS
WORTH
LOVED

```
D M F T N W C H Q N
L Y O B H D K F W P
R D K U E T R Z I M
O E L I N I R T J T
W V D X E T Y O V H
M O N N Q L A D W A
M L D R K N F I L N
W S Q L C B W V N K
G M T R E H T A F S
B E L I E V E K K Y
```

PUZZLE 37

What does the Bible say about being thankful?

1

Go into His gates giving thanks and into His holy place with praise. Give thanks to Him.
PSALM 100:4

2

In everything give thanks. This is what God wants you to do because of Christ Jesus.
1 THESSALONIANS 5:18

3

Thank God for His great Gift.
2 CORINTHIANS 9:15

4

You must keep praying. Keep watching! Be thankful always.
COLOSSIANS 4:2

5

Everything God made is good. We should not put anything aside if we can take it and thank God for it.
1 TIMOTHY 4:4

6

Let them give thanks to the Lord for His loving-kindness and His great works to the children of men!
PSALM 107:21

7

Sing the Songs of David and the church songs and the songs of heaven with hearts full of thanks to God.
COLOSSIANS 3:16

8

Always give thanks for all things to God the Father in the name of our Lord Jesus Christ.
EPHESIANS 5:20

9

I always thank God when I speak of you in my prayers.
PHILEMON 1:4

10

God is the One Who gives us power over sin through Jesus Christ our Lord. We give thanks to Him for this.
1 CORINTHIANS 15:57

Find These Words in the Puzzle!

GATES   ALWAYS   NAME
EVERYTHING   GOOD   PRAYERS
GIFT   WORKS   POWER
               SONGS

```
E V M K S R C M R G
A M B N E Q C N N R
S L A X T R M I E W
R K W N A Q H W O G
E M N A G T O R B O
Y R L H Y P K C L O
A G J R X S V F J D
R T E G I F T R K R
P V M F F L J R Q H
E M V P T S G N O S
```

PUZZLE 38

What does the Bible say about dying?

1

"I tell you, if anyone keeps My Word, that one will never die."

JOHN 8:51

2

God will free my soul from the power of the grave. For He will take me to Himself.

PSALM 49:15

3

I know that nothing can keep us from the love of God. Death cannot!

ROMANS 8:38

4

This is the reason we do not give up. Our human body is wearing out. But our spirits are getting stronger every day.

2 CORINTHIANS 4:16

5

He will take away death for all time. The Lord God will dry tears from all faces.

ISAIAH 25:8

6

If we live, it is for the Lord. If we die, it is for the Lord. If we live or die, we belong to the Lord.

ROMANS 14:8

7

"Do not be afraid of them who kill the body. They are not able to kill the soul. But fear Him Who is able to destroy both soul and body in hell."

MATTHEW 10:28

8

The last thing that will be destroyed is death.

1 CORINTHIANS 15:26

9

I heard a voice from heaven, saying, "Write these words: 'From now on those who are dead who died belonging to the Lord will be happy.' "

REVELATION 14:13

10

O death, where is your power? O death, where are your pains?

1 CORINTHIANS 15:55

Find These Words in the Puzzle!

NEVER
GRAVE
NOTHING

STRONGER
TEARS
LORD
AFRAID

LAST
HAPPY
PAINS

```
S  R  C  K  N  R  H  L  K  K
Y  T  D  I  A  R  F  A  X  M
T  R  R  N  M  D  F  G  B  M
Y  S  P  O  L  Q  S  X  E  G
P  R  A  O  N  N  X  V  B  K
P  T  R  L  I  G  A  K  R  T
A  D  P  A  J  R  E  Y  E  E
H  L  P  R  G  P  F  R  V  A
W  N  N  W  Q  L  R  M  E  R
C  N  O  T  H  I  N  G  N  S
```

PUZZLE 39

What does the Bible say about heaven?

1

The little troubles we suffer now for a short time are making us ready for the great things God is going to give us forever.

2 CORINTHIANS 4:17

2

"I will make new heavens and a new earth. The past things will not be remembered or come to mind."

ISAIAH 65:17

3

Our body is like a house we live in here on earth. When it is destroyed, we know that God has another body for us in heaven. . . . This body will last forever.

2 CORINTHIANS 5:1

4

But we are citizens of heaven. Christ, the One Who saves from the punishment of sin, will be coming down from heaven again.

PHILIPPIANS 3:20

5

"I will allow the one who has power and wins to sit with Me on My throne, as I also had power and won and sat down with My Father on His throne."

REVELATION 3:21

6

"There are many rooms in My Father's house. If it were not so, I would have told you. I am going away to make a place for you."

JOHN 14:2

7

"Gather together riches in heaven where they will not be eaten by bugs or become rusted. Men cannot break in and steal them."

MATTHEW 6:20

8

For there is no city here on earth that will last forever. We are looking for the one that is coming.

HEBREWS 13:14

9

"The ones right with God will shine as the sun in the holy nation of their Father."

MATTHEW 13:43

10

"No eye has ever seen or no ear has ever heard or no mind has ever thought of the wonderful things God has made ready for those who love Him."

1 CORINTHIANS 2:9

Find These Words in the Puzzle!

SHORT   CITIZENS   CITY
REMEMBERED   THRONE   NATION
BODY   ROOMS   WONDERFUL
                    GATHER

M	R	C	I	T	I	Z	E	N	S
D	E	R	E	B	M	E	M	E	R
N	Z	C	G	V	D	T	F	X	R
N	A	T	I	O	N	R	Z	H	O
T	P	J	D	Y	G	O	H	K	O
D	H	C	Y	A	V	H	N	Y	M
M	B	R	T	T	C	S	D	V	S
N	L	H	O	F	I	O	R	V	N
K	E	H	T	N	B	C	B	K	G
R	W	O	N	D	E	R	F	U	L

PUZZLE 40

What does the Bible say about why I'm here?

1

The last word, after all has been heard, is: Honor God and obey His Laws. This is all that every person must do.
ECCLESIASTES 12:13

2

So if you eat or drink or whatever you do, do everything to honor God.
1 CORINTHIANS 10:31

3

"Bring every one who is called by My name, for I have made him for My honor, yes, I made him."
ISAIAH 43:7

4

We are His work. He has made us to belong to Christ Jesus so we can work for Him. He planned that we should do this.
EPHESIANS 2:10

5

"This is life that lasts forever. It is to know You, the only true God, and to know Jesus Christ Whom You have sent."
JOHN 17:3

6

"Anyone who loves his life will lose it. Anyone who hates his life in this world will keep it forever."
JOHN 12:25

7

Whatever work you do, do it with all your heart. Do it for the Lord and not for men.
COLOSSIANS 3:23

8

God bought you with a great price. So honor God with your body. You belong to Him.
1 CORINTHIANS 6:20

9

"I have let you live so you could see My power and so My name may be honored through all the earth."
EXODUS 9:16

10

What does the Lord ask of you but to do what is fair and to love kindness, and to walk without pride with your God?
MICAH 6:8

Find These Words in the Puzzle!

HONOR

WHATEVER

CALLED

PLANNED

LIFE

HATES

HEART

PRICE

EARTH

ASK

P K G N X R Z R T N

R L K R T O W L V W

M D A V L N M M K R

K R M N H O R M E H

E B H A N H R V L T

P C T R L E E Q I R

M E I P D T D V F A

S L K R A M T T E E

K S X H P T R A E H

A M W C A L L E D W

Puzzle 1

```
K R K N T D F N M N
P V R H Z M H Q N N
L P X T R Y L Z G F
E K E I N L D T E V
A N M A I Q N O M Y
S J B F C A Q L O K
E M E D V E N Z H G
R F O R M W N M V L
X G E P R E A C H W
P S Y H R J Y E B O
```

Puzzle 2

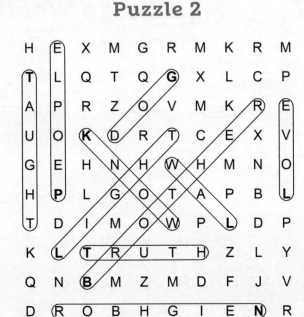

```
H E X M G R M K R M
T L Q T Q G X L C P
A P R Z O V M K R E
U O K D R T C E X V
G E H N H W H M N O
H P L G O T A P B L
T D I M O W P L D P
K L T R U T H Z L Y
Q N B M Z M D F J V
D R O B H G I E N R
```

Puzzle 3

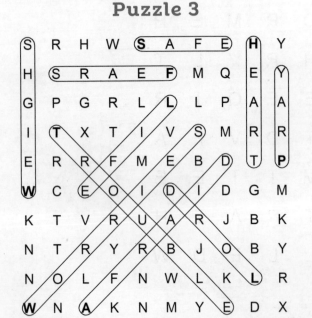

```
S R H W S A F E H Y
H S R A E F M Q E A
G P G R L L L P R R
I T X T I V S M R P
E R R F M E B D T
W C E O I D I D G M
K T V R U A R J B K
N T R Y R B J O B Y
N O L F N W L K L R
W N A K N M Y E D X
```

Puzzle 4

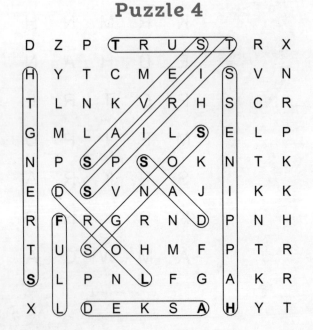

```
D Z P T R U S T R X
H Y T C M E I S V N
T L N K V R H S C R
G M L A I L S E L P
N P S P S O K N T K
E D S V N A J I K K
R F R G R N D P N H
T U S O H M F P T R
S L P N L F G A K R
X L D E K S A H Y T
```

Puzzle 5

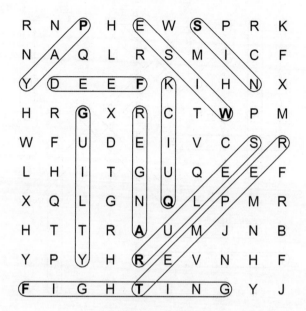

```
R  N  P  H  E  W  S  P  R  K
N  A  Q  L  R  S  M  I  C  F
Y  D  E  E  F  K  I  H  N  X
H  R  G  X  R  C  T  W  P  M
W  F  U  D  E  I  V  C  S  R
L  H  I  G  U  Q  E  E  E  F
X  Q  L  G  N  Q  L  P  M  R
H  T  T  R  A  U  M  J  N  B
Y  P  Y  H  R  E  V  N  H  F
F  I  G  H  T  I  N  G  Y  J
```

Puzzle 6

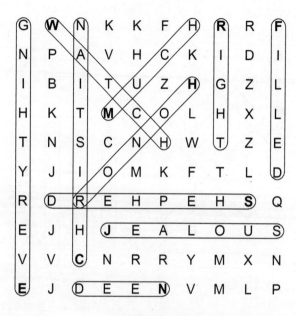

```
G  W  N  K  K  F  H  R  R  F
N  P  A  V  H  C  K  I  D  I
I  B  I  T  U  Z  H  G  Z  L
H  K  T  M  C  O  L  H  X  L
T  N  S  C  N  H  W  T  Z  E
Y  J  I  O  M  K  F  T  L  D
R  D  R  E  H  P  E  H  S  Q
E  J  H  J  E  A  L  O  U  S
V  V  C  N  R  R  Y  M  X  N
E  J  D  E  E  N  V  M  L  P
```

Puzzle 7

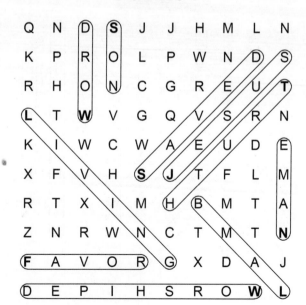

```
Q  N  D  S  J  J  H  M  L  N
K  P  R  O  L  P  W  N  D  S
R  H  O  N  C  G  R  E  U  T
L  T  W  V  G  Q  V  S  R  N
K  I  W  C  W  A  E  U  D  E
X  F  V  H  S  J  T  F  L  M
R  T  X  I  M  H  B  M  T  A
Z  N  R  W  N  C  T  M  T  N
F  A  V  O  R  G  X  D  A  J
D  E  P  I  H  S  R  O  W  L
```

Puzzle 8

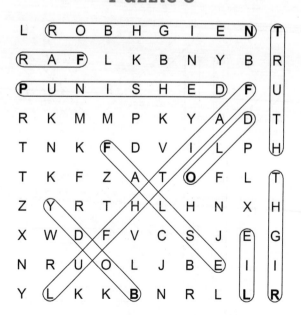

```
L  R  O  B  H  G  I  E  N  T
R  A  F  L  K  B  N  Y  B  R
P  U  N  I  S  H  E  D  F  U
R  K  M  M  P  K  Y  A  D  T
T  N  K  F  D  V  I  L  P  H
T  K  F  Z  A  T  O  F  L  T
Z  Y  R  T  H  L  H  N  X  H
X  W  D  F  V  C  S  J  E  G
N  R  U  O  L  J  B  E  I  I
Y  L  K  K  B  N  R  L  L  R
```

Puzzle 9

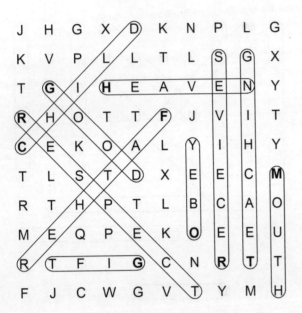

```
J  H  G  X  D  K  N  P  L  G
K  V  P  L  L  T  L  S  G  X
T  G  I  H  E  A  V  E  N  Y
R  H  O  T  T  F  J  V  I  T
C  E  K  O  A  L  Y  I  H  Y
T  L  S  T  D  X  E  E  C  M
R  T  H  P  T  L  B  C  A  O
M  E  Q  P  E  K  O  E  E  U
R  T  F  I  G  C  N  R  T  T
F  J  C  W  G  V  T  Y  M  H
```

Puzzle 10

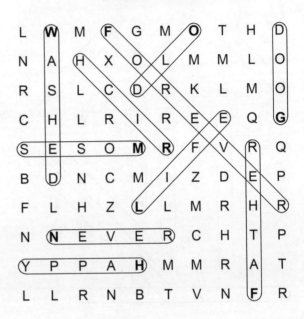

```
L  W  M  F  G  M  O  T  H  D
N  A  H  X  O  L  M  M  L  O
R  S  L  C  D  R  K  L  M  O
C  H  L  R  I  R  E  E  Q  G
S  E  S  O  M  R  F  V  R  Q
B  D  N  C  M  I  Z  D  E  P
F  L  H  Z  L  L  M  R  H  R
N  N  E  V  E  R  C  H  T  P
Y  P  P  A  H  M  M  R  A  T
L  L  R  N  B  T  V  N  F  R
```

Puzzle 11

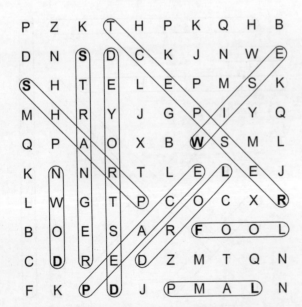

```
P  Z  K  T  H  P  K  Q  H  B
D  N  S  D  C  K  J  N  W  E
S  H  T  E  L  E  P  M  S  K
M  H  R  Y  J  G  P  I  Y  Q
Q  P  A  O  X  B  W  S  M  L
K  N  N  R  T  L  E  L  E  J
L  W  G  T  P  C  O  C  X  R
B  O  E  S  A  R  F  O  O  L
C  D  R  E  D  Z  M  T  Q  N
F  K  P  D  J  P  M  A  L  N
```

Puzzle 12

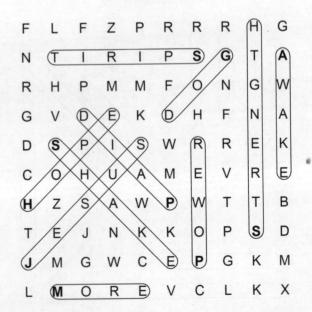

```
F  L  F  Z  P  R  R  R  H  G
N  T  I  R  I  P  S  G  T  A
R  H  P  M  M  F  O  N  G  W
G  V  D  E  K  D  H  F  N  A
D  S  P  I  S  W  R  R  E  K
C  O  H  U  A  M  E  V  R  E
H  Z  S  A  W  P  W  T  T  B
T  E  J  N  K  K  O  P  S  D
J  M  G  W  C  E  P  G  K  M
L  M  O  R  E  V  C  L  K  X
```

Puzzle 13

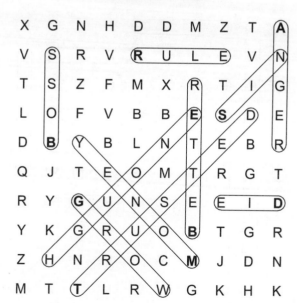

```
T Y T H A N K S M P
X T Y S H G Z G N K
D S V V L U X C K N
R N T Q V L N B W O
A I T M J S A G R W
W A P H R T N F R Y
E G R E A M T Y A Y
R A V L N L M R N B
M O K K C G P N L R
C S R E B M E M E R
```

Puzzle 14

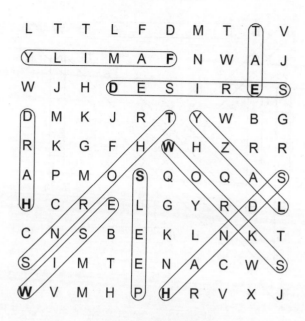

```
L T T L F D M T T V
Y L I M A F N W A J
W J H D E S I R E S
D M K J R T Y W B G
R K G F H W H Z R R
A P M O S Q O Q A S
H C R E L G Y R D L
C N S B E K L N K T
S I M T E N A C W S
W V M H P H R V X J
```

Puzzle 15

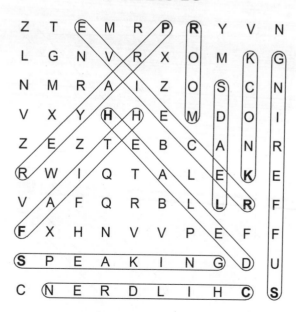

```
X G N H D D M Z T A
V S R V R U L E V N
T S Z F M X R T I G
L O F V B B E S D E
D B Y B L N T E B R
Q J T E O M T R G T
R Y G U N S E E I D
Y K G R U O B T G R
Z H N R O C M J D N
M T T L R W G K H K
```

Puzzle 16

```
Z T E M R P R Y V N
L G N V R X O M K G
N M R A I Z O S C N
V X Y H H E M D O I
Z E Z T E B C A N R
R W I Q T A L E K E
V A F Q R B L L R F
F X H N V V P E F F
S P E A K I N G D U
C N E R D L I H C S
```

Puzzle 17

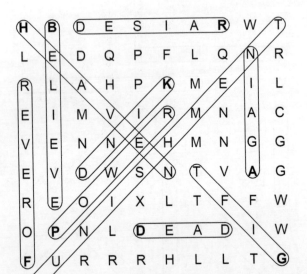

Puzzle 18

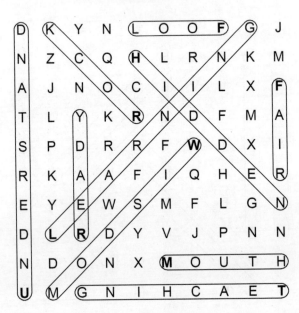

Puzzle 19

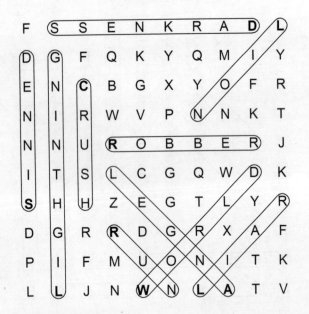

Puzzle 20

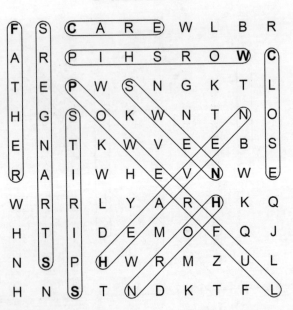

Puzzle 21

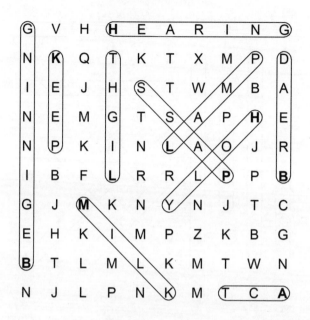

G	V	H	H	E	A	R	I	N	G
N	K	Q	T	K	T	X	M	P	D
I	E	J	H	S	T	W	M	B	A
N	E	M	G	T	S	A	P	H	E
N	P	K	I	N	L	A	O	J	R
I	B	F	L	R	R	L	P	P	B
G	J	M	K	N	Y	N	J	T	C
E	H	K	I	M	P	Z	K	B	G
B	T	L	M	L	K	M	T	W	N
N	J	L	P	N	K	M	T	C	A

Puzzle 22

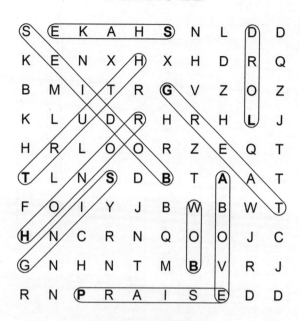

S	E	K	A	H	S	N	L	D	D
K	E	N	X	H	X	H	D	R	Q
B	M	I	T	R	G	V	Z	O	Z
K	L	U	D	R	H	R	H	L	J
H	R	L	O	O	R	Z	E	Q	T
T	L	N	S	D	B	T	A	A	T
F	O	I	Y	J	B	W	B	W	T
H	N	C	R	N	Q	O	O	J	C
G	N	H	N	T	M	B	V	R	J
R	N	P	R	A	I	S	E	D	D

Puzzle 23

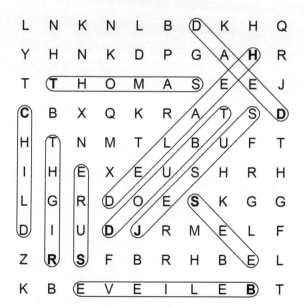

L	N	K	N	L	B	D	K	H	Q
Y	H	N	K	D	P	G	A	H	R
T	T	H	O	M	A	S	E	E	J
C	B	X	Q	K	R	A	T	S	D
H	T	N	M	T	L	B	U	F	T
I	H	E	X	E	U	S	H	R	H
L	G	R	D	O	E	S	K	G	G
D	I	U	D	J	R	M	E	L	F
Z	R	S	F	B	R	H	B	E	L
K	B	E	V	E	I	L	E	B	T

Puzzle 24

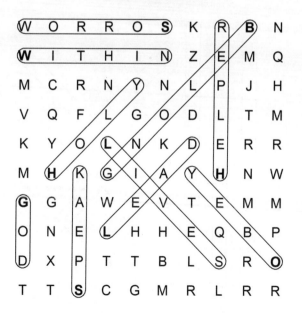

W	O	R	R	O	S	K	R	B	N
W	I	T	H	I	N	Z	E	M	Q
M	C	R	N	Y	N	L	P	J	H
V	Q	F	L	G	O	D	L	T	M
K	Y	O	L	N	K	D	E	R	R
M	H	K	G	I	A	Y	H	N	W
G	G	A	W	E	V	T	E	M	M
O	N	E	L	H	H	E	Q	B	P
D	X	P	T	T	B	L	S	R	O
T	T	S	C	G	M	R	L	R	R

Puzzle 25

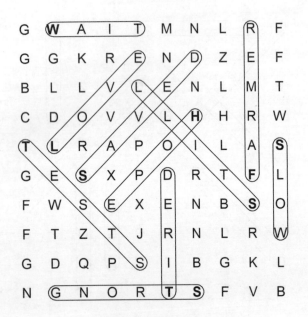

```
G W A I T M N L R F
G G K R E N D Z E F
B L L V L E N L M T
C D O V V L H H R W
T L R A P O I L A S
G E S X P D R T F L
F W S E X E N B S O
F T Z T J R N L R W
G D Q P S I B G K L
N G N O R T S F V B
```

Puzzle 26

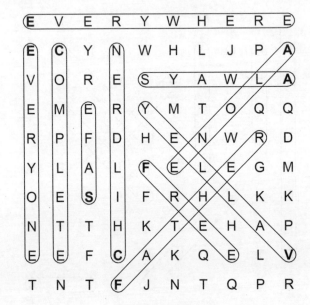

```
E V E R Y W H E R E E
E C Y N W H L J P A
E O R E S Y A W L A
V M P E R D Y M T O Q Q
R P F D H E N W R D
Y L A L F E L E G M
O E S I S F R H L K K
N T T H K T E H A P
E E F C A K Q E L V
T N T F J N T Q P R
```

Puzzle 27

```
Z H G S R B N C Y M
P S L E R E L I E M D
M E L R R V T R E Z
N T W V A G D I S P K
L E Q A F U S L N K
K L H N K I I O A T
F P T M D W L U G
D M A X J R L O T G
P O E J L W M L H Y
J C D G N I N N I S
```

Puzzle 28

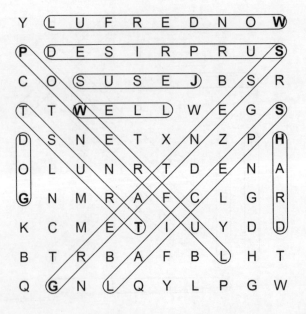

```
Y L U F R E D N O W
P D E S I R P R U S
C O S U S E J B S R
T T W E L L W E G S
D S N E T X N Z P H
O L U N R T D E N A
G N M R A F C L G R
K C M E T I U Y D D
B T R B A F B L H T
Q G N L Q Y L P G W
```

Puzzle 29

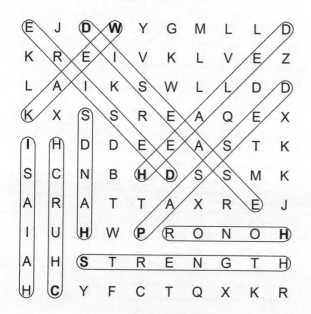

```
E  J  D  W  Y  G  M  L  L  D
K  R  E  I  V  K  L  V  E  Z
L  A  I  K  S  W  L  L  D  D
K  X  S  S  R  E  A  Q  E  X
   I  H  D  D  E  E  A  S  T  K
   S  C  N  B  H  D  S  S  M  K
   A  R  A  T  T  A  X  R  E  J
   I  U  H  W  P  R  O  N  O  H
   A  H  S  T  R  E  N  G  T  H
   H  C  Y  F  C  T  Q  X  K  R
```

Puzzle 30

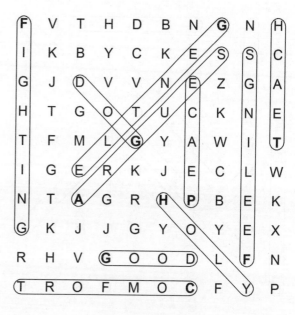

```
F  V  T  H  D  B  N  G  N  H
I  K  B  Y  C  K  E  S  S  C
G  J  D  V  V  N  E  Z  G  A
H  T  G  O  T  U  C  K  N  E
T  F  M  L  G  Y  A  W  I  T
I  G  E  R  K  J  E  C  L  W
N  T  A  G  R  H  P  B  E  K
G  K  J  J  G  Y  O  Y  E  X
R  H  V  G  O  O  D  L  F  N
T  R  O  F  M  O  C  F  Y  P
```

Puzzle 31

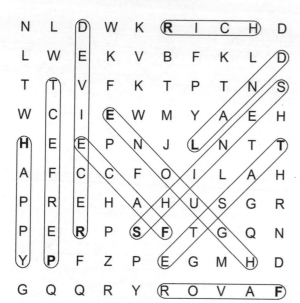

```
N  L  D  W  K  R  I  C  H  D
L  W  E  K  V  B  F  K  L  D
T  T  V  F  K  T  P  T  N  S
W  C  I  E  W  M  Y  A  E  H
H  E  E  P  N  J  L  N  T  T
A  F  C  C  F  O  I  L  A  H
P  R  E  H  A  H  U  S  G  R
P  E  R  P  S  F  T  G  Q  N
Y  P  F  Z  P  E  G  M  H  D
G  Q  Q  R  Y  R  O  V  A  F
```

Puzzle 32

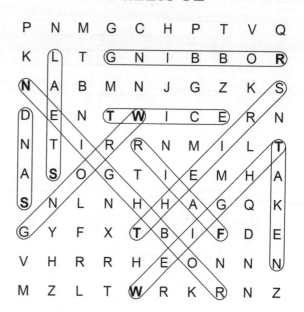

```
P  N  M  G  C  H  P  T  V  Q
K  L  T  G  N  I  B  B  O  R
N  A  B  M  N  J  G  Z  K  S
D  E  N  T  W  I  C  E  R  N
N  T  I  R  R  N  M  I  L  T
A  S  O  G  T  I  E  M  H  A
S  N  L  N  H  H  A  G  Q  K
G  Y  F  X  T  B  I  F  D  E
V  H  R  R  H  E  O  N  N  N
M  Z  L  T  W  R  K  R  N  Z
```

Puzzle 33

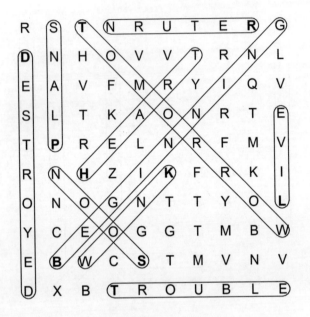

```
R  S  T (N R U T E R) G
 D  N  H  O V V  T R N L
 E  A  V F M R Y I Q V
 S  L  T K A O N R T E
 T  P  R E L N R F M V
 R  N  H Z I K F R K I
 O  N  O G N T T Y O L
 Y  C  E O G G T M B W
 E  B  W C S T M V N V
 D  X  B (T R O U B L E)
```

Puzzle 34

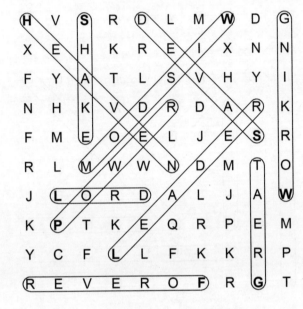

```
 H  V  S  R D L M W D  G
 X  E  H  K R E I X N  N
 F  Y  A  T L S V H Y  I
 N  H  K  V D R D A R  K
 F  M  E  O E L J E S  R
 R  L  M  W W N D M T  O
 J (L  O  R D) A L J A  W
 K  P  T  K E Q R P E  M
 Y  C  F  L L F K K R  P
(R  E  V  E R O F) R G  T
```

Puzzle 35

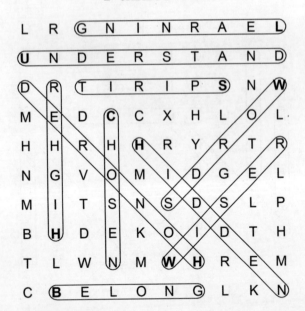

```
 L  R (G N I N R A E L)
(U  N  D E R S T A N D)
(D  R (T I R I P S) N  W
 M  E  D C C X H L O L
 H  H  R H R R Y R T R
 N  G  V O M I D G E L
 M  I  T S N S D S L P
 B  H  D E K O I D T H
 T  L  W N M W H R E M
 C (B  E L O N G) L K N
```

Puzzle 36

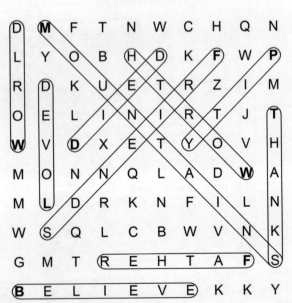

```
 D  M  F T N W C H Q N
 L  Y  O B H D K F W P
 R  D  K U E T R Z I M
 O  E  L I N I R T J J
 W  V  D X E T Y O V T
 M  O  N N Q L A D W H
 M  L  D R K N F I L A
 W  S  Q L C B W V N N
 G  M  T R E H T A F K
(B  E  L I E V E) K K Y
```

Puzzle 37

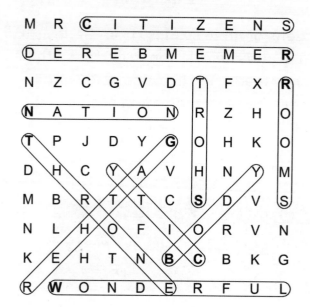

```
E V M K S R C M R G
A M B N E Q C N N R
S L A X T R M I E W
R K W N A Q H W O G
E M N A G T O R B O
Y R L H Y P K C L O
A G J R X S V F J D
R T E G I F T R K R
P V M F F L J R Q H
E M V P T S G N O S
```

Puzzle 38

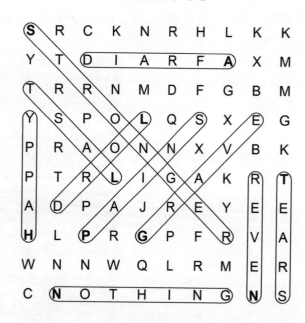

```
S R C K N R H L K K
Y T D I A R F A X M
T R R N M D F G B M
Y S P O L Q S X E G
P R A O N N X V B K
P T R L I G A K R T
A D P A J R E Y E E
H L P R G P F R V A
W N N W Q L R M E R
C N O T H I N G N S
```

Puzzle 39

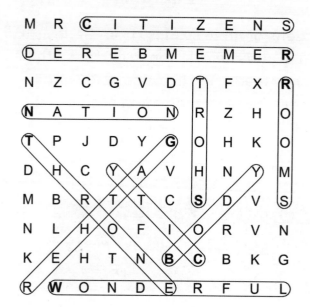

```
M R C I T I Z E N S
D E R E B M E M E R
N Z C G V D T F X R
N A T I O N R Z H O
T P J D Y G O H K O
D H C Y A V H N Y M
M B R T T C S D V S
N L H O F I O R V N
K E H T N B C B K G
R W O N D E R F U L
```

Puzzle 40

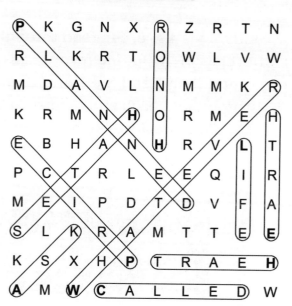

```
P K G N X R Z R T N
R L K R T O W L V W
M D A V L N M M K R
K R M N H O R M E H
E B H A N H R V L T
P C T R L E E Q I R
M E I P D T D V F A
S L K R A M T T E E
K S X H P T R A E H
A M W C A L L E D W
```

If you enjoyed
Bible Memory Word Searches for Kids. . .

Kids, ages 4 to 8, can read through dozens of Bible stories—from Genesis to Revelation—including favorites like Noah and the Ark, Jonah and the Whale, and Daniel and the Lions' Den. As they read, they'll notice bold words throughout each story—the words they'll be searching for in each puzzle. It's a great way to have fun and learn scripture at the same time!

Paperback / 978-1-63609-015-3 / $7.99